The Rebirth of the
KNIGHTS TEMPLAR,
from Jerusalem to America

NICHOLS

One Family's History

by
John A. Nichols and Myra E. Nichols

Archway Publishing books may be ordered through booksellers or by contacting:

Archway Publishing
1663 Liberty Drive
Bloomington, IN 47403
www.archwaypublishing.com
844-669-3957

ISBN: 978-1-6657-5064-6 (sc)
ISBN: 978-1-6657-5066-0 (hc)
ISBN: 978-1-6657-5065-3 (e)

Library of Congress Control Number: 2023918619

Print information available on the last page.

Archway Publishing rev. date: 10/26/2023

Contents

Acknowledgements

*To our dear family who provided
such incredible history.*

Introduction

John and I are about to share a story with our readers that will amaze and inspire you to research your family history. Knowing where you came from and learning about your ancestors really help everyone gain confidence. What you learn is that throughout history, everyone had to overcome obstacles and challenges. Maybe the time and technology was different, but people make the same mistakes and celebrate victories, just the players are different. We hope you enjoy our account of this historical journey. We sure had fun learning and writing about it, as this journey continues throughout our lives, even today.

In late December of 1997, I received a phone call from a gentleman I was hoping to hear from. We met at a family restaurant on Oracle Road in Tucson, Arizona. Our meeting led to more personal conversations, with John sharing stories about his parents and where they came from and I shared the same. I remember he spoke about Cape Cod and that his family had a large farm that at one time was nearly a section of land. He also described a cemetery with many ancestors, most he did not know. I shared my upbringing, and my Masonic family history as well as my upbringing in Job's Daughters. We discovered that we were both only children and he cared for his parents until they died. My parents had just been in a terrible car accident and I had recently moved them from California to Arizona, to care for them.

John fell in love with our small ranch in western Pima County. We had peace and quiet, yet he could commute to his job as a Conductor with the Union Pacific Railroad. The area we lived in was near an old mining community that was currently owned by Asarco of Mexico. Asarco operates a huge open pit copper mine on private land. On the north side of the Silverbell Mountains is an area near our ranch and other private land. Nearly sixty families lived throughout the private land, and we all enjoyed the wildlife, and quite a few families raised children in this paradise.

Just a few miles west of our private land, the Bureau of Land Management was opening up an area for a sand and gravel surface mining operation. The owners began their operation on ten acres, but it was planned for 900 or more acres. In only a few weeks, the blasting cracked a surface aquifer and a small lake appeared, with nearby privately owned wells going dry. We all realized that we had to stop the sand and gravel operation or we would all be out of water and the wildlife would have no place to live.

One weekend, John and I went to the sand and gravel site with some neighbors. We photographed every violation which included giant Saguaros cut in half by heavy equipment being too close to them, as well as the new lake. The area was open to the public and we never saw any signs saying otherwise. The following Monday, we took our pictures and met with the Bureau of Land Management folks in Tucson. The Manager listened to us and admitted to all the threats this operation could provide. He suggested that we either create a National Wildlife Refuge, a National Park, or a National Monument. We agreed and went home. Of course, since I had retired from the USDA Forest Service years earlier, I knew that creating any of these parks would take a miracle and an act of the President of the United States.

After we returned to our ranch, we received a phone call from a lawyer with the Pima County Supervisors. We were invited to attend a meeting and were advised that Secretary Bruce Babbitt, also our governor at one time, would be at this meeting and this lawyer, Mayveen Behan, thought we might address him about saving this area from the new mining operations. John and I were thrilled and we called some neighbors to spread the word, and the following day, we attended the meeting and presentations. The topic of the county meeting was presenting Bruce Babbitt, Secretary of Interior, with a proposal to save land in the Sonoran Desert around our ever-growing cities. After the meeting was over, Secretary Babbitt recognized my husband and came over to us. We were able to share the crisis and give him our pictures. As we left, my husband joked that he would probably be too busy to visit this area. The following morning after our newspaper was delivered, we were astonished because on the front page was a picture of Secretary Babbitt standing on the highest peak of the Silverbell Mountains, Ragged Top. He was holding our pictures and looking out over the area. We were stunned. We were later told that our meeting with him and his visit to this area saved the park and within a few months, the Ironwood Forest National Monument was created. Now, the mining industry was not happy, and litigation lasted two years, but we won. More litigation against this monument was later filed in 2016 and in 2017. I guess the 3rd time is the charm because the monument survived and our bad roads have been paved or graded. One of the species of animals that had nearly been lost was our bighorn sheep. These animals had at least eight meta populations throughout all the mountain ranges in Pima County. Due to habitat loss and over killing years ago, the bighorn sheep were gone. In the early seventies, U.S. Fish and Wildlife relocated a small herd of bighorn sheep from Yuma and relocated them in the Silverbell Mountains, but their numbers never exceeded the nineties. A couple of years before we were able to save this area, a developer brought goats into the area where the sheep lived, and the sheep contracted a disease from the goats that made them blind. We were barely at 60 sheep left when the monument was formed in 2000. The last count of bighorn sheep by U.S. Fish and

Wildlife was 435 sheep. These numbers are astonishing, and within 20 years, this population exploded. Now another group of bighorn sheep have been relocated in the Catalina Mountains and our herd is now visiting the Tucson Mountains. All the animals in the park are thriving, thanks to saving this area twenty years ago.

We shared this story about the park because it was so unusual. We were all working class people who went up against the most powerful and we won. We knew that the wildlife would be doomed. What we didn't know at that time was the history in this park, an ancient civilization that we would later write about.

John and I continued working and caring for Mom. My father only had a year with us, but it was one of his best years. Mom had ten good years of enjoying the new park, then passed. I retired from teaching at the end of the school year in 2012, and John had retired years earlier to help with Mom. By 2013, we were ready to do something fun, but we had no idea what that was.

One evening, John and I watched a program on the History Channel, with Scott Wolter, called America Unearthed. The topic was about ancient artifacts found in Tucson that suggest a Roman trading empire was here, mining gold, silver, and copper, back in 775 A.D. John and I were so excited because he had seen these artifacts years earlier and told me how special they were. When we arrived at the History Museum in Tucson, we walked into a room and in a glass case were numerous crosses and swords. Some had carvings in them, others not. John and I have been to museums and seen many ancient things, but these artifacts really hit us. We both felt goosebumps and we could not stop staring at these treasures.

The next day, John went to a used bookstore and spoke with the owner. He knew all about those artifacts and referred us to a book written by Professor Cyclone Covey of Wake Forest University. Professor Covey spent years in Arizona and at his college studying this history, and his book on the topic detailed everything. After we read his book titled *Calalus A Roman Jewish Colony in America from the time of Charlemagne Through Alfred the Great,* we were able to send him research we found on a genealogy site that identified all the kings that were here overseeing this mining operation. Dr. Covey called our research the HOLY GRAIL of Calalus. The people who came here were from the richest families of Europe. One of the kings was the grandfather of El Cid, one of the greatest Spanish warriors of all time. As we dug deeper into this mystery, more and more Roman history kept showing up. The real shock is what we found in our monument.

We joined a local archeology group and they were looking for volunteers to help them photograph and draw petroglyphs in the monument. We joined the group and were thrilled because we would learn about our home. After a few days, John called me over in private and showed me a strange cross with a medieval crown below it, pecked into a rock. The cross was quite large and the crown had great detail. We have had several experts look at this and it definitely is not Catholic. The cross is the cross of Charlemagne and the crown designates his power. Our shock and understanding of this history led to our publication in 2016, called *Calalus Revisited*. Calalus is the name of the mining colony that was here and every mountain range surrounding Tucson has evidence of ancient mining. Our rivers were massive and boats carried the ore across rivers to the Rio Grande and south to the Gulf of Mexico and east, back to Europe. We later found out that Father Kino followed the same river system when he arrived in the 1700's. Also, five tribes from the Tucson Basin and New Mexico have documented facts about these people and what they did. John and I made jokes about how easy it was for us to find the history that we did and the miracle of saving this area, but we still had no idea why things seemed to fall into place.

CHAPTER 1

Nichols Name History

The Nichols name history in Scotland begins with the Norman invasion of Briton in the early eleventh century. The Norman invasion was made up of Danish and Norwegian Vikings. A version of the Nichols' name from this region was Nicholsson. The name changed as these Normans moved throughout this region, from Britain to Ireland. Eventually, they moved into southern Scotland and the name became Nichols and was very popular. When the Normans reached northern Scotland, the name became Nicholson. There was even a Nicholson castle, located on an island off the coast of northern Scotland. Today, the castle is in ruins, and it was never rebuilt.

When we researched the family crest and coat of arms, the Scottish Nichols is different from the British and Irish, in color. The original motto of the name means *To Conquer People*. Today the motto is no longer included in the coat of arms because it is considered historical but not appropriate or too Medieval. The Danes and Norwegians were warriors and they were proud of their heritage. They married into royal families and became knights, winning battles for kings and acquiring wealth. [1]

On the top of the coat of arms is an interesting bird. This bird really surprised us for several reasons. This bird is called a Red-billed chough or Cornish chough. Their range is the coastal cliffs and mountains of the United Kingdom and Ireland to Southern Europe, Northern Africa, Asia, China and India. They are related to the C[2]row on this continent. They are highly intelligent birds and perform incredible acrobatic flight maneuvers. The other surprise was the legend of these birds. When a cornish chough dies, it joins King Arthur. This legend was fascinating.

NICHOLS

Many years ago when John worked in the railroad yard in Tucson, he saved several Ravens who were injured. Years later, he also saved a Raven near our ranch and the Raven's family lived near our home. The Ravens guard our home, notify us of visitors, and check on us throughout the day. Years ago, we visited a dear friend who lived alone, south of Tucson, Arizona. We spent the day with her and discovered a pair of Ravens had followed us to her house. To this day, those Ravens still live on her property and they have protected her many times. Those Ravens were the first and only ones she had ever seen in her area.

More recently, we sold property in Northern Arizona, in the White Mountains. We built a home and enjoyed it for 15 years, but decided to sell it. We had many Ravens visit us every time we arrived. The last day that we were there, we looked up in the pine trees and there were hundreds of Ravens in the trees. We both were brought to tears as we had no idea this would happen. We have shared some of these stories with our local Native American tribal members, and they told us we are in the Raven Clan, spiritually of course. When we read about the bird on the Scottish Nichols crest and coat of arms, we were surprised and pleased.

CHAPTER 2

Nichols Family Genealogy

In early 2017, John and I were discussing his father's love of sailing ships. He told me that his dad spent a year on an ancient looking sailing ship with the U. S. Coast Guard. I asked him why, and then he told me that his family told him that they were lowlanders of Scotland. I didn't understand so he continued with the story that they were fishermen, living on boats, making a good living. It hit me that maybe his family might be a part of Charlemagne's Rhadanite trading empire as a captain on a ship or a ship builder. He also told me that there were many generations buried at the cemetery on the farm in Cape Cod. His family knew of a connection to one of our modern day wealthy families of Europe, but no royalty. With the information on his family, we decided to investigate his genealogy. We figured why not learn about his relatives and who knows, we might get lucky with a Knight or a Captain, little did we know what we would discover.

In 2017, John and I decided to try the National Geographic genealogy test where you send in a swab and they identify noteworthy ancestors and your percentage of Neanderthal genes. When we got our results back, mine was pretty normal, a few smart people and a royal. I was thrilled. Then we looked at John's results and he had nearly 40 royals. Of course, this test reads the Y dna, the male lineage, so that also contributed to his number of royals. We definitely decided to get him tested again with the company they recommended and that was Family Tree DNA.

In 2018, we ordered a test from Family Tree DNA. The matches showed a Bishop and other names of royals, but none of the matches connected with John's family on Cape Cod. When we checked the Nichols in his matches, they were other distant relatives, none of which were from Cape Cod, Massachusetts. We later tried to get information directly through the vital records of Massachusetts or Cape Cod, but nothing was digitized and each generation would take a year. Finally, during the beginning of the Covid pandemic, we went to the vital records on Cape Cod and they were digitized. John had told me that his father's name was changed during

WWII, by accident. Of course, we later found out that not only are soldiers' names not accidentally changed by the U.S. Air Force, the process to change a name is very complex.

We may never know why his father's name was changed, but it made a difference in his genealogy search. We finally had access to the vital records of our family on Cape Cod. We now could find out when these people arrived on Cap Cod. We can also learn where they came from.

Old Sailing Ship

Our family arrived from Edinburgh, Scotland on an old sailing ship. Samuel Nichols brought his son, James A. Nichols, to Cape Cod. Samuel Nichols was born in Scotland in 1768. We were unable to get a date of his death, but he was buried in the family cemetery. After arriving, he purchased around a section of land. This farm became a two cranberry bog farm. Samuel married Sally Dutton four years after he arrived, and they shared a wonderful new life on Cape Cod, developing the farm together while living in a safe paradise.

James was born in Scotland in 1792 and died in 1900 and was buried in the family cemetery. He inherited the farm and continued the family business. His son, William Penn, born in 1850 and died in 1941, was also buried in the family plot. He not only ran the farm but also hired out as the Section Forman for the Providence Railroad. His brother became the engineer. Other family members continued the farming operations. Eventually, his son William Hall Nichols, born in1880 and died in 1957, and was also buried in the same cemetery. He continued the family business along with all the other relatives. Over time, the farm shrank and the farming changed to meet their needs.

William's son, Carmi Hall Nichols, was born in 1906 and died in 1985. He lived on the farm in his youth, but WWII took him around the world. He married and settled in the western United States, and was stationed at March Air Force Base, and lived in Pasadena, California. Carmi was transferred with a group of 30 other men, to a base near Tucson, Arizona. This base had been an old airfield prior to WWI, and became an air base during WWI. After two pilots from Tucson were killed in WWI, the Air Force honored them by naming the base after them. Samuel H. Davis and Chief Engineer Oscar Monthan would be remembered forever. [3]

The base was officially called Davis Monthan Air Force Base. Carmi and the other men in his group got the base ready for WWII. Carmi was very proud of his service, loved Tucson, and when he returned to Tucson after his service ended in WWII, he never left. Carmi joined the Pima County Sherriff Department and retired after twenty years. He also had a wonderful family, raising John Arthur Nichols.

The reason we worked so hard to identify when our family arrived and from where is due to the fact that his royal lineage includes the Knights Templars and Cape Cod has been discovered to be in their area, and we will show you in another chapter. The fact that Samuel went specifically to Cape Cod and had the resources to buy so much land and develop it seemed amazing to us. Somehow, this family had lost their history. Their royalty extends for centuries.

The rest of the chapter is a discussion and listing of all the royals in the Nichols family. Before we decided to write this book, a dear friend who retired from the French Embassy abroad begged us to write this book. She was shocked and thrilled, telling us how special this bloodline is. As Americans, it is very difficult to comprehend how significant this family history is, but we sure enjoyed researching the topic.

We now understand why we were getting so much help with the Roman history, right up through this time period. Samuel Nichols had a reason to tell the family that they were fishermen, living on their boats. He did not want their history following them to America. Now, facts are surfacing and our history is changing due to advanced technology. We now know that the folks at Plymouth didn't have the first European colony in America.

As soon as we were able to review the matches on Family Tree DNA, we looked for the oldest match. In genealogy, markers determine the time period, so we searched the oldest, the twelve marker. We noticed a bishop. He was an Episcopal bishop, of Metz. Since being a bishop sounded pretty important, we wondered if he came from royalty, and we were not surprised. Arnoldus of Saxony, Ferreolus Bishop Metz, born 565 circa was a descendant of a Roman Senator, in the southern region of Gaul that provided the Senators of Rome. Ansbertus, his father, was a Roman Senator. [4]

The next name that came up on the list is a king we are very familiar with. This king was the first king of Frankia and his efforts paved the way for his son, Emperor Charlemagne. Pepin the Short was born in714 and died in 768 circa. He conquered the Visigoths in Septimania, and became the first king of Frankia, starting the Carolegian Empire of Europe. King Pepin devoted his life to defeating the Visigoths in Frankia, and now the next bishop of Metz would be a Roman Catholic. King Pepin had opened the door, his son would rise to power, and he is the next person we discovered in the direct matches that we were familiar with. [5]

Emperor Charlemagne, or Charles I, King and then Emperor of the Holy Roman Empire of Rome. He was born April 2, 747 and died January 28, 814 circa. Charlemagne drove the Saxons out of Frankia, built roads, cities, churches, and schools. Latin became the language of Frankia and literacy returned to Europe. He rebuilt civilization and created the Holy Roman Empire of Rome in what was once Frankia.

The next king took a much longer time to figure out. After we researched the issue, we discovered that Godfrey of Boulogne, Frankia was in the bloodline of Charlemagne, his great grandfather of several generations. Godfrey was the key so we went back to the matches under the bishop, and there he was, Godfrey. Then we thought there must be more than one Godfrey, but no, only one. The story of Godfrey and his brothers was unbelievable. Godfrey of Boulogne was born in 1060 and died July 18, 1100 circa. He was the great grandson of Charlemagne. Pope Urban II ordered a military intervention in the Holy Lands over the killing of Europeans traveling to the Middle East. Godfrey was a knight and a wealthy nobleman. Godfrey and several other knights and royals answered the Pope's request. Godfrey also travelled with his brothers, Eustace and Baldwin, who were also knights, and they always fought alongside Godfrey. [6]

Godfrey became the first king of Jerusalem. Godfrey agreed to one year and quit after completing it. Then he appointed his brother Baldwin to be King. [7]

King Baldwin I of Jerusalem, was known as Baldwin of Boulogne. He was born in 1098 and ruled Jerusalem from 1100 until his death on April 2, 1118 circa. King Baldwin I focused on acquiring lands surrounding Jerusalem and along the coastal areas. When King Baldwin died, his kingdom was passed on to his first cousin, Baldwin of Bourcq, the son of Eustace, Godfrey's brother. [8]

Baldwin of Bourcq was born in 1075 and accompanied Godfrey and his brothers on the first crusade. King Baldwin II dealt with security concerns throughout the region. King Baldwin II ruled until his death on August 21, 1131 circa. [9]

King Baldwin III was the great nephew of Godfrey. He was born in Jerusalem in 1130. He ruled Jerusalem from 1143 to 1163. King Baldwin III aligned Jerusalem closely to the Byzantine Roman Empire. King Baldwin III dies in Beirut, Lebanon on February 19, 1163 circa. Baldwin III dies without an heir, so his cousin becomes the next king. [10]

Baldwin IV, great nephew of Godfrey, becomes the last European king of the Godfrey bloodline. Baldwin IV had a tragic disease that went misdiagnosed and he had to live with leprosy. He becomes known as the Leper King of Jerusalem. King Baldwin IV was born in 1161 and ruled from 1174 to his death in 1185.

Now you can understand why we were so surprised by the list of royals. Once we realized this match, we found the last one, the match we never dreamed of, the greatest king of Scotland, Robert the Bruce.[11]

Robert the Bruce, King of Scotland, is the final royal exact match. He was born on July 11, 1274 and died on June 7, 1329 circa. He ruled Scotland from 1314 until his death in 1329. [12]

What amazed us was the fact that our family only knew that they were lowlanders, with the traditional fishing career, so no questions were ever asked and no information surfaced.

We spent years researching the Roman Jews that were here in 775 circa, and we had no idea that they were family, our family. Our family was victorious in the first crusade to Jerusalem and provided 5 kings. They also created the Knights Templar and provided the most famous king of Scotland, Robert the Bruce. Of course, the early royalty of the Bishop of Metz provided all the other royals. We now agree that some of the lucky breaks we encountered along the way just might have been a lot more than lucky breaks, our family wants their story told.

CHAPTER 3

The Ancient Technolog

Antikythera Devise

We decided to devote a chapter to explain technology that was very ancient and complex, leading to technology that our ancestors used. The first object is described as an ancient analog computer, called an Antikythera devise and the other is an astrolabe. The devices were both developed by the Greeks, fifty years apart.

The Antikythera device was found on a shipwreck in 1901, near the Greek island of Antikythera. The device was identified as a mechanical device in 1902, but the device was so corroded, it was impossible to identify what it truly was. The antikythera mechanism was put in a box and shelved for decades. In 2008, scientists used surface scanning and computer X-rays to identify the lettering on the mechanism. What they discovered is that this machine was an analog computer, hand powered. This computer could predict eclipses and astronomical positions by decades into the future. The Greeks held Olympic games on the island of Rhodes. It was discovered that this device could predict the dates of these games years and months ahead. The experts believe that this computer was developed by an individual from the island of Rhodes. [13]

This mechanism contained thirty gear wheels. No other mechanism contained gear wheels until 1,000 years later, in the Medieval Mechanical Clocks. The mechanism is made of bronze sheets and would have fit in a shoebox. The doors of the front of the device and the faces are covered with Greek inscription to indicate if the purpose was calendric or astronomical. The researchers figured out that a hand held shaft that was not found, turned the main gear wheel and each revolution covered one solar year. On the front of the unit is a dial that points to the sun or the moon in the zodiac. On the back of the mechanism are two dials, the largest dial has a moving pointer showing all 235 lunations or synodic months which is approximately 19 years. The smaller dial shows four-year intervals for their Panhelenic Games, on Rhodes or at Olympia. [14]

Since the Greeks had the technology to build this computer with precise accuracy, years later, they would invent another tool for mariners on the high seas, the astrolabe.

Astrolabe

Astrolabes were invented in Greece between 250 and 150 BC. Greece was in the height of glory, considered the most important place in the world. They dominated in culture, trade, mathematics, science, philosophy, and the arts. Greece was the center of the world and their inventions changed civilization. The first astrolabe was hand held and could tell time, day or night, and pinpoint sunset and sunrise and identify celestial objects in the sky which was necessary for astrology, astronomy and most importantly, for navigation. This tool helped the ancient mariners navigate their ships throughout the Middle East and beyond. [15]

The Muslims revered the astrolabe because they could use it to determine their sacred prayer times throughout the day, and make sure they were in the correct position, facing the city of Mecca. The Arab scientists and mathematicians added their mathematical number system to the astrolabes and improved their ability for travel by sea, as the Muslim world depended on trade and with this tool, they were able to expand in any direction. [16]

Astrolabes became the IPhone of the ancient world. Today's complex navigation systems and GPS are all based on the same mathematical system used by these astrolabes. From the Phoenicians to ancient Romans, throughout the Middle East and Egypt, astrolabes helped guide these mariners all over the world. New trade routes were opened and lands explored. When the Knights Templar needed to flee into the sea, they could navigate anywhere.

By 943 circa, Muslim mariners were well aware of astrolabes. The Knights Templar lived in Jerusalem with King Baldwin II. They were in Jerusalem for decades, learning Muslim technology, finding ancient world maps from King Solomon's history, and researching everything they could so they would be effective and successful.

Now we know how a fleet of ships sailed away. On Friday the 13th, 1307, leaders and elders of the Knights Templar were arrested initially by order of King Philip IV and Pope Clement V. We were all told that everyone was rounded up and arrested, but the ships disappeared along with their treasure. Enough Knights Templar escaped to navigate those ships, and their friendliest place would be Portugal. King Denis and his family had a positive history with the Knights Templar and provided a quiet place for them to recover, rest and plan their future.

CHAPTER 4

The Knights Templar's Escape to Portugal

When the Knights Templar returned to Portugal, they needed to reinvent themselves.

King Denis of Portugal was raised around the Knights Templar and his family had always supported their efforts. Nine years after the infamous Friday the 13th, King Denis worked out a deal with Pope John XXII, requesting a new religious order be created, along with a castle and land. [17]

Pope Clement V had ordered the disbandment of the Knights Templars. The new organization would be called the Order of Christ. In 1318, the headquarters of this new organization was located in Tomar, specifically in the Tomar Castle, a Templar property from their early beginnings. The Tomar Castle ended up in the autonomous zone. The protection zone for Tomar Castle meant that all the valuables and wealth of the Templars would be transferred to the Knights of the Order of Christ. King Denis made sure that the Templars had a safe place to live. [18]

Tomar Castle and Grounds

One of the priorities of the Order of Christ was to build a navy. Portugal did not have a navy nor did they have any ships. Since the Templars had the astrolabe, they needed ships built that could handle the Atlantic Ocean. Utilizing their technology, larger ships were built and Portugal was on the map, leading exploration on the high seas. A couple of their explorers were Henry the Navigator and Vasco de Gama. In the late 14th century, Portugal was successful in employing a ship blockade in the Black Sea, destroying the spice trade and the economy of the Manluk, their old enemies who drove them out of that region when they lost the battle at Acre. [19]

The Order of Christ and the Portuguese kings were leading the world in exploration and wealth. The Order of Christ was thriving and made Portugal a global powerhouse.

Prince Henty the Navigator, Duke and Administrative General of the Order of Christ, lived from 1394 to 1460 circa. He was the first navigator who developed trade with Asia and Africa. He had his ship builders construct ships that could sail faster and carry more weight for long distance voyages. He modified the Astrolabe so his mariners had more information by providing latitude and longitude and a compass into the astrolabe. He drove the Moors out of the Iberian Peninsula and his navy travelled farther than any previous explorers. Once he had the ships that could go to the west and southern coasts of Africa, he developed a trading empire of gold and slaves, making Portugal one of the richest countries in the world. [20]

Prince Henry was not a mariner, he never sailed a ship. He provided his mariners and Portugal with marine infrastructure that made Portugal so successful, and he planned trips so Portugal got the greatest benefits.

Vasco da Gama lived from 1469 to 1524 circa and he spent his adult life dedicated to the Order of Christ. He was another incredible navigator and was able to map the nautical route to the eastern shores of Africa, and beyond to India and Asia. The Portuguese Empire expanded with his efforts. From 1497 to 1524, Vasco da Gama made four trips, securing trade, conquest, and wealth for Portugal. [21]

The Portuguese area of Tomar was a great place for the Knights of the Order of Christ to rebuild, live, and raise their families. Portugal had become a very rich nation, and the Order of Christ was very successful. In 1789, Queen Maria secularized the Order of Christ. When the monarchy of Portugal ended in 1910, the Order of Christ ended. Portugal was able to participate in international trade and negotiate treaties with other nations, along with Spain, France and England. After the monarchy ended, Portugal adopted a parliamentarian government that exists today. [22]

CHAPTER 5

The Knights Templar's Journey to Scotland and Beyond

In the previous chapter, we stated that as the Knights Templar fled France, Scotland was another option. In 1307, Robert the Bruce desperately needed help in defeating King Edward I of Scotland, an English king. If the Templars could help Robert the Bruce defeat Edward I, then Scotland would also be like Portugal, a safe haven but for very different reasons. Robert the Bruce needed their skills. The monarchy of England joined the French King Philip IV in rounding up the Templars so many English Templars fled to Scotland while others arrived on boats. [23]

All the Templars had to conceal their whereabouts while supporting and fighting for Robert the Bruce in his campaign to defeat King Edward I. Robert the Bruce was crowned king of Scotland in 1314, after the final battle at Sterling Castle. The knights raised their families and lived in peace. One of these families was the Sinclair family, William St. Clair, a Norwegian nobleman and father to Henry Sinclair, Lord of the Orkneys and Lord of Rosslyn. Henry Sinclair lived in Scotland from 1345 to 1400 circa, in the Orkney Islands. He was so respected as a mariner that his other title was Lord Admiral of Scotland. [24]

Henry Sinclair knew or had heard from other mariners that there was heavily forested land, west of Greenland. To make this journey, he needed other experienced navigators. There were two Venetian navigators, considered two of the best in the world, Nicoli and Antonio Zeno. The Zeno brothers had a great reputation. [25]

The story goes that the Zeno brothers, in 1390, followed the Viking trade routes, sailing from the North Atlantic, past Iceland, Greenland, and arriving on the shores of Newfoundland or Nova Scotia, Canada. They created a map and made extensive notes of where they stopped and identified areas and settlements along the way. The problem with this story is that their grand nephew destroyed the original map and tried to create the map from memory years later, putting most of the islands in the wrong places. In this day and age, the critics have not accepted this history at all. Recently, new research on this topic has led to a very different opinion. A report dated December 12, 2020 describes the new investigation. [26]

According to Andrea de Robulan of the American University of Rome, the notes written by Antonio and Nicoli were exact and matched everything they documented. The new investigation did not include the map because it was so wrong. Just based on their notes, the university discovered that all their documents were provable. When the Zeno brothers returned, Antonio Zeno crossed paths with Henry Sinclair. Henry Sinclair hired Antonio to be his navigator, and the map they followed was the correct map. [27]

Henry Sinclair left the Orkney Islands in Scotland and travelled 3,000 miles due west, landing in Nova Scotia with 100 men, in 1398. Henry Sinclair also had another knight traveling with him, Sir James Gunn, his lieutenant on the trip. This journey was essential to setting up a Knights Templar community, a secret community. The area could have resources for long visits, and when their work was complete, they would leave. They came here with a purpose. Years later, their secret community would provide a safe place for other Knights Templar who needed a fresh start in the New World. [28]

Henry Sinclair knew that if he just went due west from Greenland, they would run into a huge land mass. Henry Sinclair did not plan this trip for a scenic adventure. He made this journey because he had a job to complete, a place to discover, and then they returned to Scotland. The experts in Rome believe that Henry Sinclair and Sir James Gunn came here to find Oak Island. The cross that is called Fred Nolan's cross on the show called *The Curse of Oak Island*, was dated to be from 1198 circa. Henry Sinclair was on a trip to possibly bring items to be buried there.

According to Justin Forna and Emiliano Ruprah of Knights Templars in America, Season 1, Episode 3, on the Science Channel, after many weeks at sea, they finally arrived on the Canadian coast near Yarmouth and Overton. The local native tribe gathered at the shoreline, amazed to see their huge wooden ship with sails, unlike anything they had ever seen. The area where they might have arrived is where the Bay of Bundy meets the Atlantic Ocean. Evidence of their arrival has been carved in a nearby stone, 150 feet away, the Templar cross and the Mi'kmaq feather and moon. This stone is called The Overton Stone. [29]

The Mi'kmaq tribe believed that the Knights Templar needed their help and their tribe was more than thrilled to help them. They traded technology and knowledge. For the locals, this event changed their lives forever. The two groups became intertwined, as they shared information. The locals took the Templars south in the winter, following the migration of the Canadian Geese. Cape Cod, Nantucket Bay, Massachusetts, and Newport, Rhode Island were all great hunting grounds and much warmer in the winter. The tribe would migrate north in the hot summers, following their game. The two groups befriended and respected each other. The Mi'kmaq showed their respect for the Templars by making a flag that is a mirrored image of the Templar flag. They also made hats that copied the hats the Templars wore on the road to Jerusalem. Here are the two flag designs.

Flag Comparison

The top cross is the design that Henry Sinclair and his knights had on their flag, and the bottom cross design belongs to the Mi'kmaq tribe. Prior to the European arrival, the tribe didn't have a flag or hats. We were really surprised to see this cultural crossover, but it is real. [30]

According to Justin and Emiliano, they visited a gravesite of a knight that died here. In 2014, after a copy of the crest and coat of arms was discovered at the grave, the Gunn family of Europe confirmed that Sir James Gunn was buried in Westford, Massachusetts.

At the gravesite of Sir Gunn, there is a marker to another stone that was a couple of miles from this site. The stone had an ancient ship carved into it and a number of paces. When Emiliano and Justin figured out the map, they used a drone and located a stone foundation of a building, made of stone that looked identical to other Templar stonework. The site looked very undisturbed and it fit the directions on the Boat Stone.

One of the best sites in this documentary was located on a huge stone boulder that is buried with other boulders, near Newport Bridge, along Nantucket Bay and Newport. Jim Vieira, a Templar expert, pointed out carvings into this boulder that can only be seen when the tide is out, because the water is so high now. The carvings are in Latin and are the Battle Cry of Constantine, the first emperor of Rome, and the battle cry of the Nights Templars. The Latin version is *In Hoc Signo Vinces*, meaning In this sign, you shall conquer. As boats would come around a bend, they would see this giant boulder and know that they were in Templar Lands. What an incredible history lies hidden right under our feet.

The last Templar site on this documentary has to do with a tall structure right in the middle of the city of Newport, called the Newport Tower. Jim took Emiliano and Justin into the structure and the construction is amazing. The entire building is made of stone and the mortar was made from oyster shells, not concrete. This structure is not colonial. [31]

Newport Tower

This tower has been a great source of controversy. Many thought this building was a windmill, but all the windmills in the area are made of wood and designed very differently. Jim did some research to find a church that had similar stone work. Jim found a church in the Orkneys, the oldest stone church, and it just happens to be the church that Henry Sinclair visited in his youth. This church today has no roof, but the stone arches are made identical to the Newport Tower. This chuch is Eynhallow Church, built in the twelfth century and used as a monastary. The stonework and arches match the construction on the Newport Tower, it is not colonial. [32]

The Ophir Cemetary was built in the twelfth century, like the Eynhallow Church. It is made of stone and also has similar contruction style of the Newport Tower. This round cemetary is the last round cemetary standing. The stonework is very similar to the Newport Tower.

Ophir Round Cemetary

Not only has the American University of Rome supported the early arrival of Henry Sinclair in 1398 circa and the earlier travels of the Zeno brothers arriving on the Canadian shores in 1390 circa, but the Science Channel had their documentary on this topic. Also, on the last season of The Curse of Oak Island on the History Channel did their investigation. On Season 10 Episode 22, Starry Nights, Rick Lagina, Doug Crowell, Alex Lagina, and Peter Fornetti travelled to Rome, Italy and met with an Arceoastronomer, Professor Adriano Gaspanito, determine the age of the cross on Oak Island, referred to as Fred Nolan's Cross. [33]

The Arceoastronomers look at the stars back in time to determine the age of the site and they understand the alignments. The age of Fred Nolan's cross is 1200 circa. What this means is that the Templars knew of this continent and around 1198, they arrived to build the cross. Zena Halpern, who wrote the book titled The Knights Templar Mission to Oak Island and Beyond, believed that the Knights Templar arrived in America in the late twelfth century and began the work on Oak Island. [34] The stone cross was a massive challenge. The cross was perfectly aligned to constellations in the sky so the measurements had to be perfect. [35] The only devise that provided exact measurements was the astrolabe. The Templars used the astrolabe to guide their ship to Nova Scotia and Oak Island. Then they used the astrolabe to help in aligning the cross to a constellation. They might have planted the oak trees at that time as well. Also, the team on Oak Island has found similar dates on certain areas of the island, dating coal. [36]

The date on the cross is only 11 years from the fall of Jerusalem. Could the Templars have been planning this all along? If 1198 is true, the knowledge of this continent might have been passed down through our family and eventually to Godfrey. This discovery gives even more credence to the fact that his ancestors were here, and families would keep secrets like this, especially concerning lots of money or treasure.

Most of us were told that it was impossible for any country to cross the Atlantic Ocean before Christopher Columbus because of the severe Atlantic Ocean currents, and the sailors wouldn't know where they were going. Well, they all were traveling with an astrolabe, even Henry Sinclair and the Zeno brothers. Mariners communicated with each other at ports or knowledge came down through families. We believe the Roman Jews and the descendants of the Roman Seventh Legion of Septimania, Charlemagne's people, were here. We know the Vikings were here. Now we know the Knights Templar were here, a hundred years before Christopher Columbus. We now have two television networks, the American University of Rome, and members of the Vatican supporting these facts. America's obsession with keeping their old history books needs to change because this history is critical to the foundation of our country.

CHAPTER 6

Privateers and Piracy

Jolly Roger Pirate Flag

Privateering has been around as long as countries had ships and their enemies wanted their merchandise. Nations hired captains and their crews to seize merchandise and once the captain and crew got their share, the king or queen got the rest. Some privateers were more generous than others and all hired privateers worked under the protection of their rulers. For centuries, this system worked. One group who had their own navy was the Knights Templar. As early as the 13th century, some Templars worked as privateers. [37]

One famous Templar pirate was Roger de Flor. In reading about him, he had problems taking money he wasn't supposed to so the Templars made him quit the order and after Acre fell, he fled to Genoa where he borrowed a large sum of money to buy a new vessel. In 1291 circa, he is promoted to Vice Admiral by the King of Sicily to help him wage war against the French. After the war ended, Roger de Flor used his abilities to wage war on the Ottoman Turks who were battling the Byzantine Empire. Unfortunately, his greed led to his downfall and he was eventually executed by orders from the Byzantine Emperor Michael IX. [38]

Privateers continued profiting for decades, and the royals kept them busy. America depended on the privateers during the American Revolution. Over a thousand privateers were licensed by the United States and were successful during the War of 1812, against Great Briton. Due to the volume of privateers, the United States refused to sign the Declaration of Paris because without a navy, the United States depended on the privateers in time of war. All the European countries signed the Declaration of Paris, except Spain and the United States. When America developed a navy in the twentieth century, privateering was outlawed and Spain banned privateering in 1908. [39]

During migrations to America, many Knights Templar became privateers or outright pirates. If a ship was flying the jolly roger flag, everyone knew that the captain was a Knights Templar. What surprised us was how popular the pirates were in the Americas. The American colonists loved the pirates because they brought the colonists all kinds of goodies, from alcohol to jewelry, to fancy clothes, real money and the list goes on and on. The colonists looked forward to the arrival of the pirates and their governors made sure that the pirates were legally protected. From the late sixteenth to the early seventeenth century, piracy was legal and many Templars made a good living, and got out before the laws changed. Templars had the resources and the abilities to be great pirates.

One local pirate who was very popular with the colonists was Thomas Nichols, an English Nichols. Thomas Nichols was the leader of the "flying gang," operating out of Providence, Rhode Island, along the East coast, and south to the Caribbean Island. In 1717, King George offered a pardon to all pirates who surrendered before September of 1718. Thomas Nichols insisted that King George pardon other incarcerated pirates, his friends. Thomas Nichols and his friends sailed to Bermuda to Governor Benjamin Bennett's headquarters and surrendered. All of them received a pardon. [40]

Another popular pirate was Stede Bonnet. Stede Bonnet was born in Barbadoes. He inherited a large estate from his parents, but sold everything to purchase a ship and begin his new career as a pirate. He worked the East Coast and was considered a gentleman pirate. Unfortunately, Stede Bonnet crossed paths with Blackbeard. Blackbeard promised Stede a partnership and more opportunities, but during the night, Blackbeard stole his ship, along with most of his crew. [41]

Stede Bonnet purchased another ship, but was warned to stay away from the port in South Carolina. The Governor of South Carolina was determined to stop pirates from interfering with his port so he ordered a naval blockade in the area to catch any pirates who returned to confiscate his delivered merchandise. Of course, Stede Bonnet and his crew were caught and a six-hour battle ensued, with Stede Bonnet and his crew surrendering. The trial became the first of its kind in that piracy was determined to be robbery on the sea and the punishment was death. All but four of Stede Bonnet's crew were tried and executed. Stede Bonnet was then tried and was found guilty as well. He tried to get his sentence commuted, but failed and was executed on December 10, 1718. There were four members of Bonnet's crew who were released, and one of them was another Thomas Nichols who helped in the investigation. [42] Piracy continued, but certain areas were off limits, and the pirates were forced to respect the new rules.

Cape Cod currently has one of the best pirate museums in the world. Wreckage of the Whydah, a 300 year-old pirate vessel, sank off the coast of Massachusetts in a Nor'easter storm. The captain was Sam Bellamy. This ship was carrying a huge amount of treasure, so the weight of the treasure had to contribute to the sinking of the ship. All the archeological finds are recorded and displayed in the Whydah Pirate Museum. This museum has become one of the most popular tourist attractions on Cape Cod. [43]

One of the reasons piracy was so popular in the Americas was the fishing industry around Nova Scotia. Pirates found all the men they needed for crews because these fishermen could make more money working for the pirates and in between their trips, the fishermen could return to fishing. Canada's fishing industry was so plentiful that crews kept busy when their pirate ships were docked.

You're probably wondering what piracy has to do with our story of genealogy. Piracy has everything to do with it because when our family discovered piracy, in Scotland, the relatives made sure that this history was removed from the family records. These family members had no idea who they were. Nor did they understand that piracy was an acceptable career for centuries, especially if you were a Knights Templar. It was easy to destroy records in Scotland because all the birth and death records prior to 1855 were kept in parishes, and were never digitized. One phone call from a prominent family member, in the early twentieth century, could have those documents removed.

Samuel Nichols does not have a death date at the cemetery and there are no records in Scotland beyond his birth date, but with Family Tree DNA identifying the royal bloodlines and tracing our father's correct name, we can truly identify these people. Samuel brought his son, James, with him and arrived on Cape Cod in 1804. Both Samuel and James did not want their history known so they told their children that they were fishermen, which is partly true. They were also Lowlanders of Scotland, the reason their name is Nichols, not Nicholson.

The Curse of Oak Island Connection

Charlemagne's Cross

For years, we watched The Curse of Oak Island on the History Channel and the reason was the rich history. In last season 10, we finally saw the entire cross on the island, made with huge boulder alignments and the Knights Templar carvings in the rocks. We realized that what we were looking at was the Cross of Charlemagne, referred to as Fred Nolan's Cross, on the show. Now, what was the cross of Charlemagne doing at a Knights Templar site? We knew it was something significant, but we had no idea what incredible history would surface.

We began researching the topic and found that Godfrey of Bouillon was the grandson of Charlemagne by several generations, and he was one of the leaders of the first Crusade in Jerusalem. He also was a direct match to our 7th century Bishop, Arnoldus Areleous of Saxony. What made Godfrey so unique was that he never travelled without his two brothers, Eustace and Baldwin. Most royals are not that close to their siblings. Over centuries, we have all read about certain kings or queens who have had their siblings killed, to obtain absolute power. Godfrey is unique in that he kept his family by his side, throughout his life, except the last battle.

In 1095 circa, Pope Urban II called for military action in Jerusalem because the Sonjet Turkish Empire controlled the region, killing Europeans who dared to enter their realm. The Byzantine Constantinople was also under siege and had already lost territory, struggling to defend itself. When Godfrey heard the request, he liquidated all his assets. Eustace and Baldwin joined Godfrey. They recruited and trained an army. [44]

Raymond the IV, Count of Toulouse liquidated tremendous assets and recruited and trained a huge army. Other Crusader nobles and their armies included Robert II, Count of Flanders, Adhemar of Le Bohemond of Taranto, and a Norman knight from Italy. Some of the armies travelled by land, others by sea, but they all arrived at Constantinople, in stages. By May, 1097 circa, 4,000 to 8,000 mounted knights and upwards of 50,000 infantry were ready and able. In a few months, the area around Constantinople was stabilized and the Byzantine Emperor provided more infantry to help in the battles around Jerusalem. [45]

In 1099 circa, the army reached Jerusalem. Italian sailors gave up the wood from their ship to build a tall wooden tower, overlooking the [46] wall around Jerusalem. The big and last battle took place in mid July. Godfrey and his knights were the first to get over the walls and enter the city. The three-year journey to conquer Jerusalem was over and now with Christian rule, a new government had to be created. A council was formed and Count Raymond IV of Toulouse, the most royal, was offered the crown, but refused. Next was Godfrey, and he accepted. Godfrey would be the first official Christian king of Jerusalem, but Godfrey refused to be called a king because he would have to wear a golden crown and he felt strongly about Jesus wearing a crown of thorns. Godfrey changed his title to Defender or Advocate of the Church of the Holy Sepulchre and agreed to a one-year appointment. [47] Godfrey had to set up a government and protect the boundaries of Jerusalem. He also had many politics to overcome, one being who would be his successor. In a battle at the port of Acre, an Arab chronicler, al-Qalanisi documented that Godfrey was struck by an arrow that killed him, outside the city. We have read other researchers who insist that Godfrey got sick and died in Jerusalem or that he was poisoned by an enemy, but neither publication offered any details. The reason given for this controversy is that the Christian Chronicler did not document this event. [48] The Muslims knew who

Godfrey was, and we doubt that a religious chronicler would lie and make up a story of such significance. Many Muslims respected Godfrey because he tried to negotiate treaties to prevent unnecessary bloodshed. Godfrey also didn't have his brothers with him, or none of this would have happened. Since we were not there, we will leave his death to a big question. Godfrey was buried at the Church of the Holy Sepulchre. All the following kings of Jerusalem were members of Godfrey's family. Baldwin I was Godfrey's brother. Baldwin II was Eustace's son, Godfrey's nephew. Baldwin III and IV were his great nephews. Each Baldwin king stayed on the throne until he died and each king was buried at the Church of the Holy Sepulchre.

Godfrey led his knights over the wall, being the first to enter Jerusalem and he was the first ruler, setting up the government, and providing rulers for nearly 100 years. All the leaders involved in this Crusade were tremendously talented and successful, but Godfrey is the most famous. We like to think of Godfrey as a bit unique because he loved his brothers and kept them by his side, and he was very sensitive to the fact that Jesus wore a crown of thorns and not a golden crown. Godfrey absolutely refused to wear the gold crown that was made for him. He wasn't the first choice, but maybe he was the best choice because he wasn't driven by greed or power. He just wanted to do the right thing, he was proud of being a great grandson of Charlemagne. When his nephew, Baldwin II, created the Knights Templar, they changed the world.

Godfrey of Bouillon

Now we know why the Knights Templar spent so much time building Fred Nolan's Cross on Oak Island. This cross is their birthright. Without Charlemagne, none of this would have happened. Without Godfrey, there would be no Knights Templar.

At this point in this chapter, we wanted to explain the significance of the Church of the Holy Sepulchre.

Church of the Holy Sepulchre

The church was built in the 4th century, after Constantine and his army saw the ancient Latin cross in the sky and he declared Christianity the religion of the Roman world. Constantine's mother, Helena, prayed on the site of the church and experienced a deeply religious moment. Helena and Macarius found the stone that blocked the entrance to the cave were the body of Jesus was prepared for burial. Constantine built a huge church and the smaller Anastasis in the picture surrounds the tomb of Jesus and the stone that protected the entrance to the cave. The larger building is the Basilica.[49]

Once Jerusalem fell to Muslum rule, the leaders had agreed to protect all Christian religious sites. In 746 circa, the church suffered severe damage from an earthquake. Over the years, there were more earthquakes and a fire damaged the dome on the Anastasis, the small structure and then a fire in the Basilica. Finally, in 1099, the local Muslim ruler ordered the complete destruction of the church and all the surrounding buildings. Once the Crusaders arrived, what was left of the church came under protection of the Christian rulers of Jerusalem. In the mid twelfth century, the Knights Templar rebuilt the church. Throughout wars and many rulers, the Church of the Holy Sepulchre still stands. Today there are seven different religions that use this church. Last year, millions of dollars was spent rebuilding the Anastasis on the site. Countries including Jordan, Greece, and other religious organizations raised the money to make repairs on the site. In the early nineteenth century, Godfrey's grave was destroyed along with his brother and nephews, but his sword hangs on the wall inside the church. Unfortunately records did not identify the royal graves, so during outside digging, the graves were accidentally destroyed. [50]

CHAPTER 8

Where did the Freemasons Originate?

Freemasonry Symbol

Some of us have heard that Knights Templar became Free Masons, and others have heard that tradesmen and master bricklayers started the Freemasons. Most of us who have no exposure to any Freemasonry have no idea who they were because they do not advertise or promote their order. Since our families were both heavily involved in Freemasonry, we were just as curious. Our families come from the two disputed countries, Scotland and England.

After reading several conflicting articles, we finally found the Freemasonry website (Freemasonry.org) and the following information was provided by their Historical section of their Newsletter. [51]

"In 1603, James the VII of Scotland became James the I of England. Scotland and England had one monarch in the Union of the Crowns. Scotland maintained its independence. Scotland retained its own parliament, monetary system, laws, and religion. In 1536, Henry VIII abolished the Catholic Church's control over religion and he also took all of their money. During the Religious Reformation in England, King Henry VIII also abolished the guilds, small groups of similar trade workers, who would meet to discuss labor topics. [52]

In Scotland, guilds flourished because their protestant religion continued to support the guilds. In Scotland, these guilds formed incorporations by trade, from masons, carpenters, bakers, barrel makers, shoemakers, and butchers. The incorporated guilds worked more like early unions, taking care of workers' families, negotiating pay raises, and setting rules for work safety. [53]

One group of workers was considered very important and that was the stonemasons. In their time, stonemasons were at the top of the trades, and they shared many secrets that were not for public knowledge. Due to the importance of stonemasons, another layer of organization was added to the trade incorporations. The new level would provide lodges so stonemasons could meet secretly. These lodges were required to meet annually, and whenever business required urgent matters. Also, a person at each meeting had to take notes of the meetings and keep the information. The overseer to all the lodge changes was William Shaw. Shaw worked for the king and was responsible for implementing and overseeing all the new rules for the lodges. Shaw was also ordered to make all of the lodges across Scotland, permanent facilities. They would no longer be casual meeting places. Shaw made sure that all lodges held regular meetings and prior to the meetings, published the itinerary. All lodges would keep records on all activities, and they would be permanent institutions. William Shaw had already been installed and he was the first non-stonemason. Soon after the lodges were regulated, Lord Alexander, his brother, and a friend became members. When these royals were initiated at the Edinburgh Lodge, it was the first time that non-stonemasons were initiated and it was the beginning of the Freemasons of today. [54]

The controversy we ran into is that the British took credit for creating Freemasonry and they were nearly two years apart. If we hadn't read the history from the Freemason website, we would have thought the opposite. The Scottish were a couple of years ahead of England when they came to Freemasonry, but England got rid of their guilds. They had to rebuild their infrastructure so it took longer.

Freemasonry spread throughout Europe and into the colonies of America and Canada. There were royals who had relatives that were Knights Templar and their ancestors became Freemasons. Many wealthy, connected people belong to the Freemasons today. Some people believe that the Freemasons are just another extension of the Knights Templar.

CHAPTER 9

Historical Records of Freemasonry
and Knights Templars in America

We had a theory that many Knights Templar who came to America, for whatever reasons, kept quiet about their history, so a new life would be free of problems. Over the years, these same families became Freemasons and others created an American version of the Knights Templar. We found confirmation of this in historical records of the American freemasonry website and the historical Knights Templar website. We were stunned and thrilled that we now have records to prove our theory.

According to the records of the Grand Lodge of Massachusetts (Freemasonry in America.org), "the original Freemason Grand Lodge was founded in 1733. The original meetings took place at a local tavern in Boston, the Bunch of Grapes Tavern. This lodge was the third oldest in the world, following Ireland and England (which includes Scotland). The Freemasonry fraternity is now global. Men must be 18 and show good character. All religions, races, income level, educational levels, opinions, or age are welcomed. The goal is to develop people who are problem solvers, and enjoy helping others. Another goal of this fraternity is to teach leadership and responsibility." [55]

We were thrilled to find this information online. Neither of us had ever known the requirements of joining Masonry because our relatives that were Masons did not discuss the requirements, and we were so pleased to see the acceptance of races and religions, two areas that have created so much stress over the centurie.

Knights Templar Symbol

When we decided to write this book, we had no idea what facts or knowledge would surface. We had a theory from watching documentaries on the topic and discovering our family history, but the Templars in America, could that actually be real? Did they really come here to begin a new life, free of the past mistakes and disappointments? None of those knights ever thought that after they gave up all their wealth to the church, that the Pope would turn on them. We know our family was a part of this story, so we went to the American Freemasonry Website and in their historical section, we found what happened to the ancestors of the original Knights Templars who travelled to America.

The following is taken from the Masonic American, Volume II, May 1985, Devotion to Christianity, Our Temple Heritage In The United States, by Ned E. Dull, Most Eminent Grand Master from 1982 – 1985, Grand Encampment of Knights Templar in U.S.A.

"United States Templary has existed in one form or another going on 239 years. The first date of record for the conferring of the Order of the Temple in the North American continent was August 28, 1769, when Captain William Davis, Past Master, received the honor. On December 11 of that same year, Paul Revere was knighted and on May 14, 1770, General Joseph Warren received the Order of the Temple. In the early years of Templary in North America, no sovereign body was formed, and no homologous unit was achieved among the fewer than 500 known Knights throughout the colonies. In the1790's, after the Treaty of Paris was signed, the United States was looking to its future and more friendly relations with Great Britain. During this time, Templars were planning consolidation. Almost 30 years after the knighting of Paul Revere and Joseph

Warren, Thomas Smith Webb, our Templar progenitor in the United States, identified a Grand Encampment in Philadelphia, and others in Harrisburg, Carlisle, Stillwater, and New York City. In 1800 Knights Templar of New London, Connecticut, participated in the ceremonies of eulogy for General George Washington, and history records conferral of the Orders in the same year in Philadelphia and New York.

An Encampment of Knights of the Red Cross was organized in Boston in 1801. In 1802, an Encampment of Knights Templar was organized in Providence, Rhode Island. In succeeding years, new Encampments were formed in Massachusetts, Maine, Maryland, Virginia, Delaware, and other Southern and northeastern states. Knights Templary in the United States first became a supreme body in 1816. The delegates met in New York on June 20 and 21, 1816, when representatives from eight Councils and Encampments of Knights Templar and "Appendant Orders met to adopt a Constitution and to elect officers to serve until the next meeting in 1819. DeWitt Clinton (formerly a U.S. Senator and current Mayor of New York) was elected General Grand Master and was given sovereign control of Templary in the United States. Between 1816 and 1832, independent encampments consolidated under the Grand Encampment. By 1853, Templary had reached California and now spanned the entire continent. By 1856, membership had increased to 4,710 souls. Also, in 1856, The Period of Revision, William Blackstone Hubbard, the Grand Master, changed the Constitution by reorganizing the names of the groups involved, but not changing their powers. The General Grand Encampment was now to be known as the Grand Encampment, the State Grand Encampments as Grand Comanderies, and subordinate Encampments as Comanderies. From 1862 to 1874 was the Period of Civil Strife and Reconstruction. This time it was the Civil War pitting brother against brother, but the craft was in less danger of dissolution than the republic. In 1877, Thomas Edison was in his workshop, perfecting the electric light bulb and the scars of the Civil War were healing. From 1874 to 1916, was the Templar Period of Maturity, and membership just kept rising. In 1927, membership rose to 453,836. During the Great Depression, membership decreased. During WWI and WWII, membership increased substantially. Today, all over the country, Comanderies of Knights Templars meet in the Masonic Lodges."

They've evolved into problem solving organizations, teaching responsibility and leadership skills, as well as supporting local charities. Most of us have heard of the Shriners, who save lives for folks who do not have resources. The Eastern Star supports reading programs at public schools by rewarding students who improve their reading and read a record number of books, receiving a new bicycle. Years ago, educators were offered training in a new program, developed by the Free Masons, that helps teachers identify students with learning or physical challenges, and the program offers testing and resources that truly worked and helped these children. The list of charities is endless, and these people love helping their communities.

We know our family arrived on Cape Cod in 1804. We know that they came specifically to Cape Cod because they knew it was a great place for pirates and Templars. They moved here to start over, and as far as we know, they never returned to Scotland. They were proud people who chose a new beginning.

We have been researching our family for years. The name change of a significant relative was even a greater mystery. As we slowly realized the extent of royalty in this family, we developed theories of what they were up to and why. We have read many books about the Templars, but none of them were as personal, because this is our family. We never dreamed that a Masonry website would detail the American Knights Templar.

When Samuel and James arrived in Cape Cod, they had the resources to buy nearly a section of land and turned it into a very profitable double cranberry bog farm. Samuel and James knew they were getting a fresh start, and they picked an area that they felt safe in. We can only imagine if they sailed a boat around Nantucket Bay, they would've seen the giant boulder with the words, In Hoc Signo Vinces, Latin for, In this sign, you shall conquer. They knew those words very well. We hope you enjoyed this history and the rebirth of the Knights Templar.

Bibliography

Bibliotecha Planetarium. *The Arabs and the Advancement of Astrolabes.* https://www.SCIPlaet.com

Blake, Matty. *The Portugeses Connection*. The Curse of Oak Island, S9. http:THistory.com

Dafoe, Stephen. *In Hoc Signo Vinces*. Templar History. 1997. https://www.templarhistory.com

Dull, Ned E. *Our Templar Heritage in the United States*. Masonic America, Volume II, May, 1985. httsp://knightstemplars.org/knightstamplar/articles/20080316.htm

Encyclopedia.com. *Vasco de Gama*. Updated. https://www.Encyclopedia.com

Encyclopedia.com. *Prince Henry the Navigator*. Last modified on August 14, 2022. https://www.Encyclopedia.com

Encyclopedia Britannica Inc. *Antikythera Mechanism*. Last modified July 5, 2023. https://www.britannica.com/topic/Antikythera mechanism

Encyclopedia Britannica Inc. *Baldwin I*. Last modified August 28, 2023.

Encyclopedia Britannica Inc. *Baldwin II*. Last modified August 28, 2023.

Encyclopedia Britannica Inc. *Baldwin III*. Last modified August 28, 2023.

Encyclopedia Britannica Inc. *Baldw IV*. Last modified August 28, 2023.

Encyclopedia Britannica Inc. *Church of the HolySepulchre*. Last modified April 15, 2023. https://www.britannica.com/place/HolySepulchre.

Encyclopedia Britannica Inc. *Privateer*. Last modified August 2, 2023. https://www.britannica.com/technology/privat eer

Forna, Justin and Ruprah, Emiliano. *Knights Templars in America*, Unexplained and Unexplored and Unexplained, Season 1, Episode 3. https://www.Science-Channel- Unexplained and-Unexplored-2019

Freemasonry Matters. *The First Speculative Freemason*. January 22, 2019. https://freemasonrymatters.co.uk/index.php/thefirst freemason

Gonzalez, Jennifer. *Stede Bonnet and the Golden Age of Piracy*. Part Two. https://blogs.loc.gov/law/2022/12/stede-bonnett-and-the-golden-age-of-piracy-part-two/

Halpern, Zena. *The Templar Mission to Oak Island and Beyond*. Copywrite 2017.

House of Names. *Nichols History, Family Crest and Coat of Arms*. https://house of names.com/Nichols/English/product

Lagina, Rick. *Starry Nights*. The Curse of Oak Island, S10 E22. http:THistory.co

Massachusetts Freemasonry. *The Grand Lodge*. https://www.MassachusettsFreemasonry.org

The Knights Templars. *Templar Pirates*. https://www.Info_atTheKnightsTemplar.com

Tombetti, Pierluigi *The. Zeno Map and Travels of the 14th Century Venetian Zeno Brothers*. https://www.pierluigitombetti.com.zeno-map-and-travels-of-the-14th-century-venetian-zeno-brothers

Sullivan, Mike E. *Uncovering History on a 300-year–old Pirate Ship Wreakage off Cape Cod*. Reported on February 22, 2023. https:www.cbsnews.com/boston/news/escape-cod-Real-pirate--museum-Salem-massachusetts/

Wikipedia. *Arnold*. Last Modified, July 29. 2022. https://www.wikipedia.org/wiki/Arnold

Wikipedia. *Charlamagne*. Last Modified. September 2, 2023. https://www.wikipedia.org/wiki/Charlemagne

Wikipedia. *Davis-Monthan Air Force Base*. Last modified August 20, 2023. https://wikipedia.org/wiki/Davis=Monthan AirForceBase

Wikipedia. *Godfrey of Bouillon*. Last modified on September 7, 2022. http://wiki/Godfrey of Bouillon

Wikipedia. Henry Sinclair, Earl of Orkney. Last modified on August 4, 2023. https://wiki/Henry Sinclair, Earl of Orkney

Wikipedia. *Mamluk and Portugese Conflict*. Last modified on August 28, 2023. httsp://wikipedia.org/wiki/Mamluk and Portugese Conflict

Wikipdia. *Military Order of Christ*. Last modified on April 8, 2023. httsp://Wikipedia.org/wiki/Military Order of Christ

Wikipedia. *Norman Conquest*. Last modified on September 4, 2023. https://enwikipedia.org/wiki/Norman Conquest

Wikipedia. *Pepin the Short*. Last Modified September 5, 2023. https://www.wikipedia.org/wiki/PepintheShort

Wikipedia. *Red-billed chough*. Last modified on August 2, 2023. https://wikipedia.org/wiki/Red-billedchough

Wikipedia. *Robert the Bruce*. Last modified on September 5, 2022. httsp://wikipedia.org//wiki/Tobert the Bruce

Wikipedia. *Siege of Acre* (1291). Last modified on September 4, 2023. https://wikipedia.org/wiki/Seige_of_Acre

Wikipedia. *Siege of Jerusalem* (1187). Last modified on July 29, 2023. https://wikipedia.org/wiki/Seige_of_Jerusalem

Wikipedia, *Thomas Nichols (pirate)*. Last modified June 30, 2023. Httsp://Wikipedia.org/wiki/Thomas Nichols(pirate)

Endnotes

1   House of Names, *Nichols History, Family Crest and Coat of Arms*, p. 1-3.

2   Wikipedia, Red-billed cough, p. 1.

3   Wikipedia, *Davis-Monthan Air Force Base*, p. 3-5.

4   Wikipedia. *Arnold*, p. 1.

5   Wikipedia. *Charlamagne*, p. 1.

6   Wikipedia, *Godfrey of Bouillon*, p. 1-2.

7   Wikipedia, *Godfrey of Bouillon*, p. 2.

8   Encyclopedia Britannica Inc. *Baldwin I, p. 1-2.*

9   Encyclopedia Britannica Inc. *Baldwin II, p. 1-2.*

10 Encyclopedia Britannica Inc. *Baldwin III, p. 1-2.*

11 Encyclopedia Britannica Inc. *Baldwin IV, p. 1-3.*
     Wikipedia, *Robert the Bruce*, p. 1-3.

12 Wikipedia, *Robert the Bruce*, p. 4.

13 Encyclopedia Britannica Inc. *Antikythera Mechanism, p. 1.*

14 Encyclopedia Britannica Inc. *Antikythera Mechanism, p. 1-2.*

15 Bibliotecha Planetarium. *The Arabs and the Advancement of Astrolabes, p. 2.*

16 Bibliotecha Planetarium. *The Arabs and the Advancement of Astrolabes, p. 2-3.*

17 Wikipedia, *Military Order of Christ*. p. 1-2.

18 Wikipedia, *Military Order of Christ*. p. 2-3.

19 Wikipedia, Mamluk-Portugese Conflict. p. 1-2.

20 Encyclopedia.com. *Prince Henry the Navigator,* p. 1.

21 Wikipedia, History of the Order of Christ, p.4-5.

22 Encyclopedia.com. *Vasco de Gama*. p. 1.

23 Wikipedia, *Robert the Bruce*, p. 1-3.
     Wikipedia, *Robert the Bruce*, p.

24 Wikipedia, Henry Sinclair, Earl of Orkney, p.1.

25 Tombetti, Pierluigi *The. Zeno Map and Travels of the 14ᵗʰ Century Venetian Zeno Brothers*, p. 1-2.

26 Tombetti, Pierluigi *The. Zeno Map and Travels of the 14ᵗʰ Century Venetian Zeno Brothers*, p. 1-2.

27 Tombetti, Pierluigi *The. Zeno Map and Travels of the 14th Century Venetian Zeno Brothers*, p. 1-2.

28 Forna, Justin and Ruprah, Emiliano. *Knights Templars in America*, Unexplained and Unexplored and Unexplained, Season 1, Episode 3.

29 Forna, Justin and Ruprah, Emiliano. *Knights Templars in America*, Unexplained and Unexplored and Unexplained, Season 1, Episode 3.

30 Forna, Justin and Ruprah, Emiliano. *Knights Templars in America*, Unexplained and Unexplored and Unexplained, Season 1, Episode 3

31 Forna, Justin and Ruprah, Emiliano. *Knights Templars in America*, Unexplained and Unexplored and Unexplained, Season 1, Episode 3.

32 Forna, Justin and Ruprah, Emiliano. *Knights Templars in America*, Unexplained and Unexplored and Unexplained, Season 1, Episode 3

33 Lagina, Rick. *Starry Nights.* The Curse of Oak Island, S10 E22.

34 Halpern, Zena. *The Templar Mission to Oak Island and Beyond.* p. 259.

35 Lagina, Rick. *Starry Nights.* The Curse of Oak Island, S10 E22.

36 Lagina, Rick. *Starry Nights.* The Curse of Oak Island, S10 E22.

37 Encyclopedia Britannica Inc. *Privateer*, p. 1.

38 The Knights Templars. *Templar Pirates*, p. 2.

39 Encyclopedia Britannica Inc. *Privateer*, p. 1.

40 Wikipedia, *Thomas Nichols (pirate)* p. 1.

41 Gonzalez, Jennifer*, Stede Bonnet and the Golden Age of P.racy*, Part Two, p. 1.

42 Gonzalez, Jennifer*, Stede Bonnet and the Golden Age of P.racy*, Part Two, p. 2.

43 Sullivan, Mike E. *Uncovering History on a 300- year –old Pirate Ship Wreakage off Cape Cod*, p. 2.

44 Wikipedia. *Godfrey of Bouillon, p. 4.*

45 Wikipedia. *Godfrey of Bouillon, p. 4.*

46 Wikipedia. *Godfrey of Bouillon, p. 6.*

47 Wikipedia. *Godfrey of Bouillon,*p. 9.

48 Wikipedia. *Godfrey of Bouillon,*p.10.

49 Encyclopedia Britannica Inc. *Church of the HolySepulchre*, p.1-2.

50 Encyclopedia Britannica Inc. *Church of the HolySepulchre*, p. 1-2.

51 Freemasonry Matters. *The First Speculative Freemason*, p. 1-2.

52 Freemasonry Matters. *The First Speculative Freemason*, p.2.

53 Freemasonry Matters. *The First Speculative Freemason*, p. 2-3.

54 Freemasonry Matters. *The First Speculative Freemason*m p. 3-4.

55 Massachusetts Freemasonry, *The Grand Lodge*, p. 1.

Printed in the United States
by Baker & Taylor Publisher Services